WILD ANIMALS

CHIMPANZEES

BY DALTON RAINS

WWW.APEXEDITIONS.COM

Copyright © 2026 by Apex Editions, Mendota Heights, MN 55120. All rights reserved. No part of this book may be reproduced or utilized in any form or by any means without written permission from the publisher.

Apex is distributed by North Star Editions:
sales@northstareditions.com | 888-417-0195

Produced for Apex by Red Line Editorial.

Photographs ©: Shutterstock Images, cover, 4–5, 6–7, 10–11, 12, 13, 16–17, 20, 21, 24, 25, 26, 29; iStockphoto, 1, 8–9, 18–19, 22–23; Anup Shah/Nature Picture Library/Alamy, 14

Library of Congress Control Number: 2024952637

ISBN
979-8-89250-546-8 (hardcover)
979-8-89250-582-6 (paperback)
979-8-89250-650-2 (ebook pdf)
979-8-89250-618-2 (hosted ebook)

Printed in the United States of America
Mankato, MN
082025

NOTE TO PARENTS AND EDUCATORS

Apex books are designed to build literacy skills in striving readers. Exciting, high-interest content attracts and holds readers' attention. The text is carefully leveled to allow students to achieve success quickly. Additional features, such as bolded glossary words for difficult terms, help build comprehension.

CHAPTER 1
CHIMP ATTACK 4

CHAPTER 2
AMAZING APES 10

CHAPTER 3
CHATTY CHIMPS 16

CHAPTER 4
LIFE CYCLE 22

COMPREHENSION QUESTIONS • 28
GLOSSARY • 30
TO LEARN MORE • 31
ABOUT THE AUTHOR • 31
INDEX • 32

CHAPTER 1

CHIMP ATTACK

A chimpanzee **patrol** moves through the forest. The chimps hear an unfamiliar call. A **rival** group is eating from a fig tree. The patrol sneaks closer. Then they attack!

Chimpanzees usually make lots of noise. But they stay silent before an attack.

The attacking chimps bite and kick. The rival group tries to fight back. But there are too many attackers.

FAST FACT
Chimps may throw rocks or branches during fights.

A chimp has sharp teeth near the front of its mouth.

Soon, the rival group scatters. The attackers have a new food source. The chimps climb up the fig tree and start eating.

TAKING OVER

Male chimps often walk along the edges of their group's **territory**. They keep other chimps out. And they search for places to attack. That way, the attacking group can get food from the new areas.

The territory of a chimpanzee group usually covers 4 to 15 square miles (10 to 40 sq km).

CHAPTER 2

AMAZING APES

Chimpanzees live in central and western Africa. Most chimps grow between 3.2 and 5.5 feet (1 and 1.7 m) tall. The apes can weigh 71 to 132 pounds (32 to 60 kg).

A chimp's body has brown or black hair. The animal's hands, feet, and face are mostly hairless.

Chimps often swing through the trees from branch to branch.

Chimps are strong. They have long arms, long hands, and long fingers. These features help chimps climb trees.

FAST FACT
Chimps usually walk on all fours. But they can also walk upright.

On the ground, chimps can run 25 miles per hour (40 km/h).

Chimps are omnivores. The apes prefer fruits and plants. But they also eat insects and eggs. Chimps may even hunt other animals.

SUPER SMART

Chimps often use simple tools. The apes use sticks to dig up insects. They use leaves and moss to make sponges. Chimps even use certain plants as medicine.

Chimps sometimes use rocks to break open nuts.

CHAPTER 3

CHATTY CHIMPS

Chimpanzees are social animals. The apes live in groups. Some groups have fewer than 20 chimps. Others have more than 100. Each group has a male leader.

16

Chimps may fight one another to become the leader of a group.

Chimps make **alliances** with other members of their group. An alliance may help the current leader. Or it may try to put a new chimp in charge.

DIFFERENT STYLES

Chimps have different personalities. Some leaders are **aggressive**. They use their strength to stay in control. Other leaders are friendlier. They may groom other chimps to form bonds.

Chimps often pick out insects and dirt from one another's hair.

Chimps have big ears. That helps them hear other chimps in thick forests.

Chimps **communicate** with sounds. They use **gestures**, too. For example, a chimp may show excitement by stomping and screaming.

FAST FACT
Chimps also communicate with their faces. They sometimes laugh or smile.

Chimpanzees sometimes hug and kiss one another.

CHAPTER 4

LIFE CYCLE

Chimpanzees can **mate** at any time of year. A mother gives birth eight months later. She usually has just one baby.

A newborn chimp weighs about 4 pounds (1.8 kg).

Mother chimps cuddle and play with their babies.

A chimp is helpless at birth. It drinks milk from its mother for about four years. The mother cares for the young chimp for up to 10 years.

STAYING CLOSE

At first, a baby chimp clings to its mother's belly. Later, it rides on her back. The young chimp learns to walk after a few months. But it learns from its mother for years.

Even adult chimps spend lots of time with their mothers.

A male chimp usually stays in the group he was born in. A female usually joins another group. There, she has babies of her own.

FAST FACT
Chimps are fully grown after 13 to 16 years.

◀ Wild chimps live about 45 years. As they age, the apes get gray hair and go bald.

COMPREHENSION QUESTIONS

Write your answers on a separate piece of paper.

1. Write a few sentences explaining the main ideas of Chapter 3.

2. Which feature of chimpanzees do you find most interesting? Why?

3. For how long does a young chimp drink milk from its mother?
   - **A.** eight months
   - **B.** four years
   - **C.** 45 years

4. Which chimp would be most likely to lead a group?
   - **A.** a strong male
   - **B.** a very young male
   - **C.** a small and weak male

5. What does **omnivores** mean in this book?

*Chimps are **omnivores**. The apes prefer fruits and plants. But they also eat insects and eggs.*

    A. animals that eat only plants
    B. animals that eat only animals
    C. animals that eat both plants and animals

6. What does **personalities** mean in this book?

*Chimps have different **personalities**. Some leaders are aggressive. They use their strength to stay in control. Other leaders are friendlier.*

    A. ways of climbing
    B. ways of acting
    C. ways of eating

Answer key on page 32.

GLOSSARY

aggressive

Strong and quick to attack.

alliances

Groups of animals that work together.

communicate

To pass on information.

gestures

Body movements.

mate

To form a pair and come together to have babies.

patrol

A group that travels together to keep watch over an area.

rival

Having to do with a group that fights or competes with another group.

territory

An area that an animal or group of animals lives in and defends.

BOOKS

Klepeis, Alicia Z. *Jane Goodall*. Abdo Publishing, 2022.
Mattern, Joanne. *Chimpanzees*. Bellwether Media, 2021.
Temple, Colton. *Chimpanzees*. Kaleidoscope, 2022.

ONLINE RESOURCES

Visit **www.apexeditions.com** to find links and resources related to this title.

ABOUT THE AUTHOR

Dalton Rains is an author and editor from Saint Paul, Minnesota.

INDEX

A
Africa, 10
alliances, 18

B
babies, 22, 25, 27

C
climbing, 8, 12
communicating, 20–21

F
forest, 4

G
groups, 4, 6, 8–9, 16, 18, 27

L
leaders, 16, 18–19

M
mating, 22

O
omnivores, 15

P
patrol, 4

T
territory, 9
tools, 15
trees, 4, 8, 12

W
walking, 9, 13, 25

ANSWER KEY:
1. Answers will vary; 2. Answers will vary; 3. B; 4. A; 5. C; 6. B